PROSTHODONTICS MANUAL FOR PRECLINICAL STUDENTS-COMPLETE DENTURE

VARSHA RAJEEV

Copyright © Varsha Rajeev
All Rights Reserved.

This book has been self-published with all reasonable efforts taken to make the material error-free by the author. No part of this book shall be used, reproduced in any manner whatsoever without written permission from the author, except in the case of brief quotations embodied in critical articles and reviews.

The Author of this book is solely responsible and liable for its content including but not limited to the views, representations, descriptions, statements, information, opinions and references ["Content"]. The Content of this book shall not constitute or be construed or deemed to reflect the opinion or expression of the Publisher or Editor. Neither the Publisher nor Editor endorse or approve the Content of this book or guarantee the reliability, accuracy or completeness of the Content published herein and do not make any representations or warranties of any kind, express or implied, including but not limited to the implied warranties of merchantability, fitness for a particular purpose. The Publisher and Editor shall not be liable whatsoever for any errors, omissions, whether such errors or omissions result from negligence, accident, or any other cause or claims for loss or damages of any kind, including without limitation, indirect or consequential loss or damage arising out of use, inability to use, or about the reliability, accuracy or sufficiency of the information contained in this book.

Made with ♥ on the Notion Press Platform
www.notionpress.com

To All My Students

Contents

Preface   *vii*

Contents   *ix*

  1. Impression Compound   1

  2. Pouring The Casts   9

  3. Custom Trays & Denture Bases   15

  4. Occlusion Rims   20

  5. Articulation   26

  6. Teeth Arrangement   31

  7. Wax Up, Root Carving, Festooning & Sealing   38

  8. Cast Separation & Flasking   41

  9. Dewaxing & Packing   43

  10. Acrylisation, Deflasking, Finishing& Polishing   45

References   47

Preface

This book is a humble attempt to make the lives of young dental students just a little bit easier. Most are thrown into the world of dentistry at the young age of eighteen with little to no knowledge of what this field entails and the work that goes into completing the course. More often than not, students are overwhelmed by the myriad of information they are expected to absorb almost immediately, and apply to their practical exercises. The second year of this course is particularly taxing in the sense that students have a lot of theoretical data to learn as well as a lot of practical exercises to complete in order to be eligible for their university examinations.

Pre clinical Prosthodontics is a major source of stress among dental students. The curriculum is both fast paced and challenging. The students are expected to develop skills of manual dexterity, orientation, precision and attention to detail in order to keep up with the deadlines. A lot of the time, students face frustration, dejection and burn out during their second year. It is all new to them, and one cannot really fault the students for feeling these emotions.

Every student is different and possesses a unique aptitude for the course. To expect all students to be equally adept at the various preclinical Prosthodontics exercises is not only unrealistic, but it is also unfair. This book has attempted to address some of the roadblocks that students may face while trying their hand at these exercises. Although there isn't much detail about the theoretical aspects of the materials, I have tried to take a more practical approach to the subject and have tried to explain some of the queries that students might have.

Knowing that this book has many aspects that can be improved upon and that there will be better editions of the same in future, I sincerely hope that this book will be of some help to the students. If I can help at least one person, I will consider myself a good teacher.

Varsha Rajeev

Contents

CHAPTER 1: Impression Compound

CHAPTER 2: Pouring the Cast

CHAPTER 3: Special Trays and Denture Bases

CHAPTER 4: Occlusion Rims

CHAPTER 5: Articulation

CHAPTER 6: Teeth Arrangement

CHAPTER 7: Wax Up, Carving and Sealing

CHAPTER 8: Dental Cast Separation and Flasking

CHAPTER 9: Dewaxing and Packing

CHAPTER 10: Acrylisation, Finishing and Polishing

REFERENCES

CHAPTER I

Impression Compound

I remember when I first entered the preclinical laboratory and saw metal dies of edentulous arches and cakes of impression compound. I was so confused! Nobody taught us what exercises we were doing, why we were doing them or how these exercises would help us in our clinical practice. For that matter, nobody bothered to tell us what dental material we were using either. Let's change that shall we?

Why do you need this exercise?

The first clinical step when making a complete denture is to make a primary impression. In order to develop our impression making skills, we are made to practice on edentulous dies that simulate an edentulous patient's maxillary and mandibular arches. The material we are initially introduced to in the subject of Dental Materials, apart from Dental Plaster, is probably Impression Compound. A thermoplastic rigid impression material, this is very commonly used to make primary impressions for edentulous patients and therefore, this is an important preclinical exercise.

So the preclinical exercise is to make a primary impression of an edentulous maxillary and mandibular arch using impression compound. This involves using softened impression compound in an edentulous impression tray and recording the impression of the die. Let's dive into it!

What materials do you need?

1. Edentulous maxillary arch and mandibular arch models

2. Rubber bowl
3. Gauze
4. Hot water
5. Impression compound
6. Edentulous impression trays
7. BP blade and handle
8. Spirit lamp or blowtorch
9. Chip blower
10. Mackintosh sheet

So the first thing you want to do after arranging your instruments on your mackintosh sheet is select your impression tray. Make sure the tray is covering all the anatomical landmarks and there is a 2mm to 3mm space between the tray and the die. This space is for the impression compound material that will be placed in the tray before making the impression. Since these trays are stock trays, you may not get a perfect tray fit. You can adjust the tray using orthodontic pliers to improve the adaptation of the tray and you can also trim the tray if it is in excess anywhere using a metal file or metal trimming burs.

Once the tray is selected, the next step is to manipulate the impression compound.

How do I manipulate impression compound?

To manipulate impression compound, take the rubber bowl and fill it with hot water. Not boiling water, hot water. You want the temperature of the water to be around 60 degrees Celsius. How will you know, right? It's not like you are carrying a thermometer in your pocket!

So here's a tip: if you can dip your finger in the water for more than 10 seconds, it's NOT hot enough. There's no point in immersing your impression compound in lukewarm water and wasting time. You will never get the consistency that you need for a good impression. You also want to make sure that the water is not boiling hot. This will alter the properties of the impression compound and hence the quality of the impression. Once the hot water is in the bowl, place a gauze piece within the bowl.

The gauze piece will help you handle the softened impression compound easier. Once softened, it may stick to the rubber bowl, making the next step difficult. A piece of gauze placed in the bowl helps by acting like a barrier between the impression compound and the surfaces of your rubber bowl.

Next, take a cake of impression compound and break it into halves or quarters so that it fits easily into the bowl. Place it over the gauze piece and let it sit under water till it softens.

How do you check whether the impression compound has softened?

Wait for about two to three minutes. Take any instrument you have at hand like a Lecron's carver or the blunt end of your BP handle and gently poke the impression compound to determine that it is softened all the way through its mass. The next step is kneading. Remove the softened mass out of the bowl by lifting up the gauze piece and knead it with your hands. You want to get a homogenous mass that is softened equally throughout without any lumps.

For how long can you knead?

Remember now, this is a thermoplastic material and so, is completely temperature dependant. Do not knead for more than 10 to 15 seconds to avoid the re-hardening of the impression compound. Place it back into the rubber bowl for a few seconds if you feel the material needs to soften again for further manipulation. Keep checking the temperature of the water to make sure it hasn't cooled down. Be sure to change it if it has.

Once you are sure of the homogeneity of the material, keep the bowl aside and roll the softened impression compound quickly into a ball for a maxillary impression or a cylinder for a mandibular impression.

How do you record the impression?

Place the shaped impression compound into the respective impression tray. Gently press the impression material into the tray spreading the material and rolling it slightly over and beyond the borders of the impression tray. Be careful not to press too hard. This will cause thinning of the impression compound and you may not get a well recorded impression. Make sure there are no folds in your impression material during this step as they will remain there after recording the impression as well. If you find folds, remove the material and repeat the step after softening again.

Once you have adapted the material onto the tray, you may notice the impression compound has begun to harden. Place the impression tray with the impression material in it back into the rubber bowl to soften it for a few seconds. Do not place it for too long otherwise the material will go beyond the consistency required for a good impression and may even dislodge from your tray. Also ensure while you are dipping the tray, that the impression material does not stick to the sides of the rubber bowl.

The next step is recording the impression. So first you want to orient your impression tray correctly over your die. Align the labial notch of your impression tray to the labial frenum of the die to make sure it is centred correctly. Apply downward pressure perpendicular to the primary stress bearing areas for about 10 seconds. You will notice some excess material rolling out from the sides of the impression tray. This is good and is to be expected. Gently adapt this impression material over the die from the posterior end of the die to the anterior. This ensures that the impression material covers all the anatomic landmarks and flows anteriorly covering the rest of the landmarks as you go.

Make sure this excess is adapted onto the land area of the die and the borders of your impression tray to avoid its fracture during impression retrieval.

Another factor to check is whether your impression tray is parallel to the tabletop or floor. You can check this by making sure the handle of your impression tray is parallel to the floor or tabletop after positioning your tray on the die.

How much is too much?

Take care not to apply too much pressure while making the impression. Remember that the impression compound is soft and will yield to any pressure applied. Too much pressure will cause perforation of your impression and exposure of your impression tray. You want to press down on the tray such that you can see the impression compound slowly roll out from the edges and then stop. When the material rolls out, it is already indicative of overall contact with the die surface, so you don't need more force.

Once you have made sure the tray is centred correctly and parallel to the floor, apply gentle and stable pressure mainly over the hard palate for maxillary impressions and over the buccal shelf area for mandibular impressions. The reason is because these areas are the primary stress bearing areas for their respective arches, which means these areas are biologically designed to take on stress. Once you have adapted the excess or removed it if it was too much, wait for the material to set. Now how long do you wait? Well it really depends on the temperature again. Wait for the material to cool down to room temperature. This could take a few minutes. Gently press down on the sides of the excess impression material after two to three minutes and check if it is still soft. Once the borders have hardened, touch the centre of your impression tray to make sure it has cooled down as well. Then with a gentle but firm motion, remove the tray from the die and assess your impression.

1. Have you recorded all the anatomic landmarks?
2. Have you made sure that the impression tray is not exposed anywhere?
3. Is the impression centred over the impression tray?
4. Is your impression free of folds or any other irregularities?
5. Has the land area of the die been recorded evenly throughout your impression?

If you have answered yes to these questions, chances are your impression is acceptable. If you find minor errors, you can re heat your impression compound in hot water or using a spirit lamp and chip blower or a blowtorch to soften the localised faulty area of your impression. Make sure you show your teacher before deciding to re-record any areas. Major errors may warrant repeating the impression procedure.

What if you have corrections to make in the impression?

Reheating the impression in hot water is pretty much the same procedure. Dip the area you wish to record again in hot water and wait for the material to soften. Once it is soft, place the impression tray back onto the die and apply pressure. Wait for the material to set and assess your impression.

If you are using a sprit lamp or a Bunsen burner and chip blower, do be careful not to burn yourself. Hold your impression in one hand and the chip blower in the other hand on either sides of the flame. Gently blow the flame with the chip blower on to the area of interest. Remember that this is fire so the impression compound will heat up much faster than when immersed in hot water. So, just a few seconds will do.

To repeat the impression completely, place your impression with the tray in your bowl of hot water and wait for the compound to soften. When it softens, you can easily remove the impression material from your impression tray and repeat the procedure.

How do you trim the excess material?

If your impression has been approved, your teacher will probably ask you to trim the excess material. Now depending on your preclinical exercise, you have to decide how much to trim. If you have to preserve the land area for further exercises, then do not encroach into the land area portion of your impression. If not, then you may trim off the land area portion of your impression up till the curvature of the flange of the impression.

So how do you trim excess impression compound? Well if there is a lot, you can first grossly trim the excess by heating the excess area to soften them and then slice them off with a BP blade. Take note that this is only for gross trimming. For finer trimming it is safer to just shave off the excess. Hardened impression compound will flake off when you run the blade against the area to be trimmed.

Trimming while preserving the land area is actually easier as you just have to follow the margins. If you have to trim off the land area then you have to be careful not to trim off the necessary portions of your impression. So remember to go slow. Trim off the land area and once you reach the impression, follow the shape of the flange. Don't trim the superior borders of the flange. Stick to the outer portions of the land area till you reach the flange and then stop. Show your teacher regularly to make sure you are on the right track. Once you are done, check to see the borders of your impression are smooth and even.

And you have completed this exercise. Great job!

CHAPTER II

Pouring the Casts

Why do you need this exercise?

Once your impressions are made, the next exercise would be pouring a cast from the impressions obtained. In a clinical scenario too, after making the primary impression of the patient, you are required to pour the primary cast using dental plaster. You may already be familiar with dental plaster as most curriculums encourage making free forms using dental plaster so as to acclimatise you to the material.

What materials do you need?

For Inversion Method:

1. Rubber bowl
2. Straight spatula
3. Lecron Carver
4. Plaster knife
5. BP blade and handle
6. Ceramic tile/ glass plate
7. Sand and/or emery paper
8. Mackintosh sheet

For Beading and Boxing Method:

1. Modelling wax sheets
2. Spirit lamp or Bunsen burner
3. Wax spatula
4. Wax knife
5. Rubber bowl

6.   Straight spatula
7.   Lecron Carver
8.   Plaster knife
9.   BP blade and handle
10.   Ceramic tile/ glass plate
11.   Sand and/or emery paper
12.   Mackintosh sheet

Now to pour the cast, there are essentially two techniques which I will be discussing here:

1.   INVERSION METHOD:

How do you pour the dental plaster in the impression?
In this method, first make a smooth creamy mix of dental plaster. Pour some of the mix into the impression. Start from one end and gently tap the impression on the table or use a vibrator machine to move the mix along the surfaces. Cover all surfaces of the impression and bulk it up in height about an inch. Set it aside without tilting and make some criss-cross striation marks along the dental plaster to give a source of mechanical retention.

How do you pour the base?
Next, mix dental plaster but make sure it is not too loose in consistency. This is for the base of the cast. Place the mix on a tile or glass plate and give it an arbitrary cast base shape. You can use instruments like your plaster knife, Lecron carver etc. You can even use a wax knife, but make sure you don't use it for manipulating wax after that!

How do you invert the impression into the base?
Once the base has been shaped, take the impression in which the plaster you placed earlier would have reached its initial set. Now invert it over your base and press down

in the palatal region mildly, just enough to observe the dental plaster from the base portion get pushed upwards and outwards. Now start shaping the land area for your cast. Remove any excess dental plaster and add on wherever necessary till you get a good base and a neat and uniform land area. For this, you can try using an instrument like a Lecron's carver, plaster knife, dedicated wax knife for dental plaster work, BP blade or even your own finger tips dipped in water. As long as you get the desired shape and size, it is my personal opinion and suggestion that you use any instrument that gets the job done. Just be mindful not to use instruments for wax and dental plaster. If you are using an instrument for wax procedures, do not use them for dental plaster procedures as well. Always have dedicated instruments and of course, follow any explicit instructions your teacher gives you. You can keep some extra land area, maybe around 8mm so that when you trim the base of the cast you won't end up trimming off the land area as well.

How do you retrieve the Primary Cast?

Once the plaster is set, place your cast with the impression tray embedded in it into a bowl or container of hot water. This will soften the impression compound and enable you to retrieve the impression tray from the cast. Remove all remnants of the impression compound from the anatomic portion of the cast gently taking care not to scrape of any of the anatomical features you have recorded. Trim off the excess cast base both width and height. Make sure your primary cast is at least 15mm at the thinnest portion so that it doesn't break easily.

While making the mandibular cast, special attention should be given to the tongue space area. Make sure it's smooth and flat and blends with the rest of the cast. Keep this in mind while arbitrarily shaping the base. Make sure there is enough material there before inverting the impression into the base.

You can use abrasive papers like sand paper or emery paper to polish your cast when you are done trimming.

1. BEADING AND BOXING METHOD:

Why learn this method?

This method is commonly used to pour master casts after making secondary or master impressions. You may however have a preclinical exercise where you are required to pour a pair of casts from primary impressions made without the land area recorded. The main advantage of this method over inversion method is the land area. You are creating land area while beading and this will preserve the important details of the flange of the impression and therefore the sulcus.

How do you make beading strips?

For beading, take strips of modelling wax, if beading wax is unavailable. Let the strips be about 10mm wide. Heat them over a flame and fold them in half so you now have strips of 5mm width.

How do you bead the impression?

Heat a strip again and when softened, adapt the strip along the flange of the impression about 2mm below the superior border of the flange. Follow the outline of the flange while adapting the wax strip. Using strips of smaller length helps you handle them better. The trick is, when the wax is soft, you must adapt it quickly before the wax cools down and hardens again. The soft wax will stick to the impression compound easily. Once you are happy with the positioning of the wax strip, seal the margin between the beading and the impression with the help of a wax spatula. Remember, this step can feel frustrating because of the quick cooling and hardening of modelling wax. But don't worry, we have all been there. Take your time, take smaller lengths of wax strips if that makes it easier for you and don't forget to seal each strip well before proceeding to the next. You've got this!

For the maxillary impression, the posterior beading will be at the level of the impression. For the mandibular impression, cut a sheet of wax and adapt it in the tongue space region. Take care that the beading in the posterior portions of the mandibular impression is not inclined otherwise the land area of the cast you pour will also be inclined. You can modify the width of the beading with the help of a wax knife or a wax spatula if you feel the width is more in certain areas.

After beading, make three wax stumps and adapt them onto the underside of the impression tray in a tripod fashion so that the impression will be parallel to the floor or the table when it rests on the stumps.

How do you box the impression?

To box the beaded impressions, take a sheet of wax, soften it and adapt it to the beading all around. You may need two sheets for boxing. After adapting the wax, do seal the junctions properly to ensure that the dental stone will not flow through while you are pouring the cast. You can check by pouring a few drops of water to check for leaks.

How do you pour the cast?

When the beading and boxing is deemed satisfactory, mix dental stone, again, taking care that it's not too thin or thick, and pour it into the boxed impressions in increments making sure to coat the surface of the impression using a vibrator machine or gently tapping it. Once the cast is set, gently remove the wax with any instrument and carefully remove the impression tray as discussed earlier with hot water.

Since the cast is made after the impression was beaded and boxed, you won't have much trouble finishing the casts. Still, you can use the BP blade or a Lecron carver to finish the cast and modify the land areas where necessary. Any excess can be trimmed off using the stone trimmer. Sand paper and emery paper can be used to polish the casts and this exercise is done.

Good job getting this far!

CHAPTER III

Custom Trays & Denture Bases

Why do you need this exercise?

By now, you may have finished pouring master casts with dental stone. The next exercise may be to fabricate denture bases using self cure acrylic resin material. Or it may be to fabricate special trays on your primary casts. So let us discuss the general technique for both under this section. Clinically speaking, you will need to know the techniques for fabricating special trays for making secondary impressions as well as denture bases for recording the patient's jaw relation.

What materials do you need?

1. Plastic dispenser bottle for polymer
2. Syringe for monomer
3. Rubber bowl
4. Lecron carver
5. Pencil
6. Red colour pencil
7. Blue colour pencil
8. Separating media
9. Camel's hair brush
10. Porcelain jar

Before making the special trays, first you need to mark three lines on the primary casts. One line with a graphite pencil to mark the deepest part of the sulcus on your cast, one line in blue colour 2mm above the line that depicts sulcus depth which signifies the border of the special tray, and a final line in red 4mm above the sulcus depth line which signifies the border of the spacer.

The spacer outline will depend on the spacer design that has been chosen. Your teacher will guide you in selecting a suitable spacer design, so you needn't worry about it.

How do you apply separating media?

Before getting into the HOW, let's just go over the WHY. Why do we need a layer of separating media? The simple answer is that we need to be able to remove the finished acrylic tray or denture base from the cast when it is done. Without a layer of separating media, the acrylic will react with the underlying cast making separation nearly impossible without destroying the cast. Applying a layer of separating media will create a barrier film between the cast and the acrylic tray or denture base, so don't forget to apply it!

First apply separating media on the casts. Make sure you apply a coating with a camel's hair brush or a piece of cotton drenched in separating media and held with tweezers. Apply separating media in a single direction to avoid disrupting the layer that may be forming on the surface of the cast.

Once the separating media is dry, heat, soften and adapt wax over the dental cast. Then proceed to cut away the excess wax till the spacer outline drawn by you. Cut about 2mm by 4mm rectangles of spacer wax out in the areas of the tissue stops as well. Seal the boundaries of the wax spacer to ensure it stays in place while making the special tray.

Any precautions to take before you start working with acrylic material?

Before beginning, do wear a mouth mask as monomer fumes are harmful for health. It is also safer to use gloves while working with acrylic to avoid allergic reactions.

There are two methods commonly used to fabricate acrylic appliances: the Dough Method and the Sprinkle-On Method. The Dough Method basically involves manipulating the acrylic material into a dough consistency and then moulding it into the shape of a tray by adapting it on the cast. This is however a bit difficult to do especially if you are starting out, so mostly, your teacher is going to show you the Sprinkle On method which involves sprinkling some acrylic polymer on to the cast and then adding drops of acrylic monomer over the powder so that it becomes moist and acrylizes. This incremental technique albeit slower, gives you more control over what you are doing and is great for beginners.

So in the Sprinkle On Method, starting from one end, dispense some polymer onto the surface of the cast. Then inject a few drops of monomer using a disposable syringe. You can bend the needle of the syringe for better access. Continue this process and cover the entire outlined area of the special tray. Any excess material that flows out of the lines can be removed with a Lecron carver. Dipping the tip of the carver in monomer will prevent the acrylic from sticking to the carver. That way, when you are cutting away the excess, the tray material will not come along with it. Make sure the thickness of the tray is at least 2mm all over.

What to do during polymerisation?

Once you have finished applying the material, wait for the polymerisation reaction to take place. Cover the cast with a rubber bowl to avoid rapid evaporation of monomer. After a few minutes, remove the bowl and separate the tray from the cast by gently teasing the sides with an instrument. The tray should separate from the cast without much difficulty.

How do you check the tray or denture base thickness?

Check the thickness by placing it in the path of light. If any translucent areas are seen, then chances are the tray is thin in those areas and you may need to add more material. Adding material is the same procedure. To increase thickness in areas that don't involve the border, you can just add more polymer and monomer. If the area you want to accentuate involves the border, then make sure you apply another coat of separating media first to avoid any difficulty in removing the special tray or denture base after.

You can then trim off the excess in the acrylic trimmer. If you are fabricating a special tray, then the tray handle and finger rests can be attached on the tray. Handle should be 3mm to 4 mm thick, 8mm to 10mm long and 8mm to 10mm wide. You can mix the polymer and monomer in a porcelain jar with a lid and when dough consistency is reached, which will take roughly 10 minutes, mould the material into the desired shape and size and adapt it onto the tray. Smoothen the edges with the help of monomer.

Finishing and polishing can then be done. After gross trimming of the acrylic, you can use acrylic burs, sandpaper and/or emery paper, felt cones and pumice and rag wheels to polish the surface of the tray.

Difference between fabrication of special trays and denture bases?

For making denture bases, the procedure is essentially the same. The denture base will extend into the depth of the sulcus, however. While trimming, make sure you don't trim too much material from the sulcus area. Be sure to preserve the depth and width of the denture base flange.

What can you do about porosities?

Porosities are a very common issue while dealing with acrylic resin material. Some things to look into while using this material are:

1. Make sure the cast is dry and only then is separating media applied onto the dry cast.
2. Make sure that the coat of separating media is dry before making the special tray or denture base.
3. Do not allow monomer to evaporate rapidly. Place a rubber bowl over the cast while working.
4. Make sure monomer is not deficient while using sprinkle on technique.

If you have followed all these guidelines, chances are your special tray and denture base will be approved by your teacher. Good Job!

CHAPTER IV

Occlusion Rims

I remember dreading the days when we had to make occlusion rims. I had no idea what to do with all that wax! And don't even get me started on the measurements! Mine were invariably 1mm short. And when I attempted to add wax, I would end up losing the occlusal plane or there would be a cant. In short, it was a nightmare.

Why do you need this exercise?

The truth of the matter is, you absolutely need to learn how to make occlusion rims. Clinically, you will need to record the patient's jaw relation with the help of the occlusion rims. So faulty occlusion rims will land you in a lot of trouble. As for the measurements, you need to be trained in precision. In your patient's mouth, you may need to modify your occlusion rims by a few millimetres. Developing that skill now will help you in your clinical future.

What materials do you need?

1. Modelling wax sheets
2. Rubber bowl
3. Hot plate
4. Wax knife
5. Lecron carver
6. Glass plate
7. Metallic scale
8. Bunsen burner or spirit lamp
9. Chip blower or blow torch
10. Cotton

11. Mackintosh sheet

Once you have arranged all the instruments, the first thing you need to do is draw reference lines or guidelines on the master cast.

For the manidibular cast:

1. The retromolar pad area is marked and is divided into three parts: anterior one-third, middle one-third and posterior one-third. The height of mandibular posterior occlusion rim should be at the level of the junction of anterior two-thirds and posterior one-third.
2. The posterior extent of the mandibular rim should be limited to the anterior aspect of the retromolar pad.
3. The crest of the alveolar ridge is marked and is extended posteriorly and anteriorly on to the land area, which serves as a guideline for fabrication of the occlusion rim. The width of the posterior occlusion rim should be equidistant or equal on either side of the crest of the ridge.

For the maxillary cast:

1. Mark the maxillary tuberosity of the cast.
2. Mark the anterior border of the tuberosity on the land area of the cast.
3. Mark the incisive papilla.
4. Mark the midline of the cast by connecting midpalatine raphe, incisive papilla and the labial frenum. Extend this line to the land area of the cast.
5. Draw a perpendicular line to the midline through the centre of the incisive papillae and extend it to the land area and this line is called canine–papilla–canine (CPC)

line. The midline, CPC line and limiting of the posterior extent of maxillary occlusion rim are visible on the land area following placement of adapted denture base.

After drawing the guidelines, place the denture base over the cast and make sure the markings on the land area are visible. Now we can start fabricating the occlusion rims.

How should you soften wax for the occlusion rim?

Take a sheet of modeling wax and heat it over the flame. As the wax softens, roll it up along its breadth. Make sure the wax sheet is closely adapted while doing so to avoid air bubble entrapment.

How do you adapt the softened wax on the denture base?

After rolling the wax, adapt it onto the denture base. Start from one end and follow the arch form all the way to the other end. While adapting the wax, build up the height as you go with your fingers, adapting the wax onto the labial and palatal surfaces as well.

Roughly create the anterior proclination as well. Make sure you are following the arch form while doing this. It is easier to modify the shape and position of the occlusion rim at this stage rather than

Once the wax has cooled down and hardened. Cut off the posterior excess beyond the anterior border of the maxillary tuberosity. For the mandibular occlsusion rim, the posterior limit of the rim should not cross the anterior limit of the retromolar pad and the posterior height not beyond the anterior two-thirds of the pad. The rough shape of the occlusion rims are ready.

How do you shape the occlusion rims further?

Seal the borders of the occlusion rims on to the denture base with a heated wax knife and slope the posterior aspect of the maxillary rim. Measure the height of the occlusion rims. Usually it will be more than necessary. For the maxillary arch, the anterior height from the deepest part of the sulcus should be 20mm to 22mm and in the molar region around 18mm. for the mandibular rim, anteriorly 16mm to 18mm and posteriorly up to the anterior two-thirds of the retromolar pads.

Using an instrument, mark the excess wax to be removed with the help of the metallic scale. Then using the heated hot plate, carefully run the occlusion rim over the hot plate till the desired wax height is achieved. Remember to go slow and not incline your hand as you don't want to reduce too much wax. It is always easier to remove wax than add wax on the rim. And make sure you do this over a bowl filled with water otherwise you will end up with a mess of wax everywhere.

Re check the height with the scale. Next place the occlusion rim on the glass plate to check the plane. Place only the occlusion rim without its cast. The weight of the cast may alter the plane of the rim when placed on the glass plate.

When placed on the glass plate, the occlusion rim's plane should be parallel to the glass plate. If there is a cant, there may be a disparity in the anterior or posterior heights of the occlusion rim. Do not apply force while checking the occlusal plane as this will also alter the rim height. Make sure you hold the denture base in the region of the hard palate for the maxillary occlusion rim and make sure the retromolar pad areas of the mandibular occlusion rim do not touch the glass plate to avoid any errors in checking the plane and height of the occlusion rims.

What do you do if there is a cant?

First things first, measure the height again with the scale. If you find that there is a lack of height anywhere, you will have to add wax. If on the other hand, there is an excess in height, that area will have to be reduced.

In the case of excess height, mark the excess on the rim, reduce the height in that region with a wax knife or a selectively heated hot plate taking care not to touch the other areas of the occlusion rim and then check the height again. Once the height is satisfactory, place the rim on the glass plate and check its plane. If there is a slight gap anywhere, smooth it over by adding drops of wax.

In case of deficient height, add wax in the area required. Wax can be added either by melting wax with a heated spatula and applying it on the rim, alternatively you can roll up some was and melt it over a flame and pace the resulting drops of melted wax on the required areas. Always add more wax than necessary. This is because, after adding wax you will have to run the hot plate over it to smoothen the surface of the occlusion rim. Some excess wax allows room for this step. Otherwise, you are back where you started. After adding wax and smoothening the surface, check the occlusal plane again for any gaps or cants. More often than not, you will get it right in a few tries. If not, don't worry. As you work on it more, you will get the hang of it. Just be sure to stay patient and focused as it's easy to get frustrated.

Next check the width of the occlusion rims. Width anteriorly should be 4mm to 6mm and posteriorly 6mm to 8mm. Up to 10mm is also acceptable. Once both rims are fabricated, bring them together in occlusion and make sure there is even contact between the planes of both rims and there should be an overlap of the maxillary rim over the mandibular rim labially as well as buccally. If there are any gaps between the rims, wax will have to be added there. But those will only be minor adjustments. Also smoothen the labial and palatal or lingual surfaces of the occlusion rims. You can use a heated hot plate or wax knife for this.

How do you remove air bubbles?

If there are any air bubbles, they have to be removed. Using a heated wax spatula or wax knife, break the air bubble and while the wax is still molten, add a drop or two of melted wax and smooth it over. Now you can polish your occlusion rims. Using a chip blower and flame or a blowtorch, heat the surface of the occlusion rim to be polished carefully. Do not overheat and melt the rim you worked so hard to fabricate! Just a mild application of heat to melt the surface of the rims which looks like the wax has become cloudy. Then using a piece of cotton soaked in water, run it over the surface of the occlusion rim and you will see a polished shiny wax surface.

Now you can get the rims approved by your staff, mark the midline, and transfer it to your casts. You have made your occlusion rims.

Congratulations!

CHAPTER V

Articulation

Now that you have your occlusion rims ready, the next major exercise would be articulation. Before this step of course, you will have to index your master casts. Indexing involves making 'V ' shaped notches or ridges across the base of your casts in order to aid in mechanical retention of your cast to the articulation as well as aid in re-orienting the casts after processing the complete dentures. Since this step is not usually problematic, it has not been dealt with.

After indexing the casts, approximate them together by aligning the posterior walls of both cast bases on a flat surface or table-top. After getting approval for this from your staff, seal the occlusion rims together in the molar area with a heated wax knife. Make an 'X' mark on both sides of the occlusion rims to seal the maxillomandibular relationship in place.

Why do you need this exercise?

Articulation is an important laboratory step after recording the patient's jaw relation. This step essentially transfers the patient's jaw relation to the mechanical device i.e the articulator. Although you don't really record the maxillomandibular relation because you're doing purely preclinical exercises which do not involve patients, you still need to get the hang of all these procedures before you begin doing patient cases, because any errors in these procedures could jeopardise the clinical success of the prosthesis.

Before you begin, make sure your articulator does not have a rotated incisal pin, make sure the vertical rod is flush with the upper member and that there are no inherent cants in your articulator. Your teacher will help you with this.

How to check the thread relation?

The next step is thread relation. Here you have to orient the casts within the articulator such that the occlusal plane is essentially centred between the upper and lower members of the articulator. You can use wax stumps for this step. So what all do you look for in this step?

1. The vertical rod should be in contact with the incisal guide table.
2. The incisal pin should be pushed in completely and should just be in touch with the anterior border of the maxillary occlusion rim.
3. The maxillary cast's posterior border should be parallel to the posterior border of the upper member or the posterior reference rod.
4. The thread when drawn from one end of the posterior reference rod to the other, must be equidistant from the casts and rims and must be in line with the occlusal plane.

What do you do if the vertical rod is not touching the incisal guide table?

Well this happens if the upper member is hitting the maxillary cast, in which case you will have to reduce the height of the anterior wax stump.

What is wrong if your incisal pin is not pushed in completely?

The position of the incisal pin determines the position of the maxillary central incisors and the anterior occlusal pane. If the pin is not pushed in completely, then after articlulation, any change in the position of the pin will alter the position of the maxillary anterior teeth which is not ideal.

You also need to check whether the incisal pin is at the same level as the maxillary occlusion rim. If the pin is above, the height of the anterior wax stump needs to be reduced, and if the pin is below, the height of the anterior wax stump needs to be increased.

If the maxillary cast is not parallel to the posterior border of the upper member or the posterior reference rod?

That means the cast is rotated. Either the casts have been sealed wrong, or their relationship has altered during thread relation procedure or the maxillomandibular assembly has been rotated as a whole. Correcting the maxillary cast automatically centres the entire assembly.

What do you do if the thread is above the line of the occlusal plane?

This means that the height of the posterior wax stumps has to be increased. And if the thread is below the line of the occlusal plane, then the height of the wax stumps has to be reduced.

What do you do if the thread is below the line of the occlusal plane?

This means that the height of the posterior wax stumps has to be reduced.

When all conditions are met and the thread relation has been approved by your staff, you can proceed with articulation.

What materials do you need?

1. Rubber bowls
2. Straight spatula

3. Lecron carver
4. Wax knife(used solely for gypsum product manipulation)
5. Plaster knife
6. Mackintosh sheet

How do you articulate the maxillary cast?

The first step is to open the upper member of the articulator and apply a coat of petroleum jelly or other separating media on the notches made in the maxillary cast. This is to enable its easy separation before processing.

Next mix dental plaster into a smooth creamy mix. Apply this mix first into the notches of the maxillary cast. Then apply the rest of the mix onto the flat base of the maxillary cast following the borders of the cast. Close the upper member. Ensure that the vertical rod is in contact with the incisal guide table and the incisal pin is in the same relation as earlier obtained. The plaster will flow into the spaces of the upper member.

Now shape the borders of the articulation following the shape of the maxillary cast. It helps if you have an extra bowl with water to remove the excess plaster from the articulator. You may use a plaster knife or a wax knife for this step. Be careful while removing excess from the posterior aspect. Do not alter the thread relation. Make sure to check occasionally that thread relation is being maintained. If there are any deficiencies, add plaster in those areas. You may use the excess plaster you removed earlier for this. Try to get smooth sharp edges that mimic the shape of the cast.

How do you articulate the mandibular cast?

Once the articulation of the maxillary cast is done, wait for it to reach initial set before proceeding with articulation of the mandibular cast. A small weight or elastic band can be placed over the articulator while the plaster sets to counter any plaster expansion.

Now invert the articulator carefully. Open the lower member and gently remove the wax stumps. Repeat the procedure done for the maxillary cast articulation here as well. Don't forget to check the thread relation here too. Any change in thread relation warrants repetition of this entire step.

You can smoothen the surface of the set dental plaster using sand and/or emery paper. Wash the articulator to free it of any dental plaster debris and dry it thoroughly. Check the thread relation one final time to ensure that your thread relation is still intact and correct. If there is any change you will have to repeat the exercise because during the teeth arrangement process, your thread relation will be the only guide you have to check your occlusal plane. If your thread relation is correct after articulation, then Articulation is done!

CHAPTER VI

Teeth Arrangement

The articulated casts are now ready for the next step which is teeth arrangement.

Why do you need this exercise?

Teeth arrangement is one of the pillars for denture esthetics and function. Lack of knowledge about how to arrange the individual teeth will prove to be disastrous for the patient. Since the principles of teeth arrangement have been well documented and discussed in many text books, we won't be repeating that here. Instead, let's look at the common mistakes and oversights and see their potential solutions.

Before beginning with the teeth arrangement, open up the articulator. This will break the seal made between the occlusion rims. In the mandibular cast, the crest of the ridge has already been marked on the land area. Extend this line onto the posterior aspect of the cast. Close the articulator and turn the articulator to view the posterior aspect. Extend the line you just marked on the mandibular cast onto the posterior aspect of the maxillary cast. And continue this line onto the land area of the maxillary cast. This will serve as a guideline while arranging the maxillary posterior teeth.

What are the common errors students make while arranging the maxillary anterior teeth?

1. Forgetting to transfer the midline:

Always transfer the midline from the occlusal rim to the master cast either with a pencil or a thin marker tip. During teeth arrangement, you will be manipulating the occlusion rim a lot and it's easy to lose the midline marked in the rims. Transferring on to the master cast is the safest way to avoid midline shift during teth arrangement.

1. Forgetting to check the incisal in position:

While arranging the maxillary anteriors, we will have to pull out the incisal pin to a certain extent to get space to remove and place the occlusion rims on the maxillary cast. But in the midst of all this, when checking the anteroposterior position of the maxillary anterior teeth, aways push the incisal pin in completely. Otherwise you risk incorrectly placed maxillary anterior teeth which may cause errors in mandibular anterior teeth arrangement as well.

3. Forgetting to tilt the lateral incisors:

This error which is quite common is mainly because we forget the principles of teeth arrangement. The maxillary lateral incisors are to be arranged slightly tilted towards the distal at the cervical third. This enables the incisal edge to be parallel to the glass plate. The cervical third of the lateral incisor is also pushed in deeper than that of the central incisor to get a 20 degree inclination labially. This is also often overlooked during teeth arrangement.

4. Maxillary canine position:

The maxillary canines are very important in giving esthetics to the teeth arrangement. There are many things to keep in mind regarding these teeth. There will be a distal rotation. When viewed from the front they will be distally tilted or parallel to the long axis. When viewed from the side they will be straight. The cervical third will be prominent. This is also very important to highlight the maxillary canines and contribute to esthetics.

5. Glass plate relation:

When placing the maxillary occlusion rim on the glass plate, always hold it in the centre of the hard palate. If you press down on the anterior portion of the denture base it will appear as if the glass plate relation is correct when in fact it may not be. Always make sure that when the occlusion rim is placed on the glass plate: the maxillary central incisors, the maxillary canines and most importantly, the rest of the occlusion rim is contacting simultaneously. If only one tooth is contacting, it is probably out of the occlusal plane and its position should be modified to be within the occlusal plane.

What are the common errors students make while arranging the mandibular anterior teeth?

If the maxillary anterior teeth are properly arranged, we can use them as a guide while arranging the mandibular anterior teeth. Here are the common errors:

1. Midline shift:

Despite transfer of the midline to the casts, midline shift errors can still occur. This may be due to movement of the teeth during arrangement due to excess force applied or due to lack of proper sealing of the tooth in the wax. You can check for a midline shift by viewing the teeth from the posterior aspect. When viewed from the palatal aspect with the rims occluded, one should be able to see a diamond shape forming whilst opening and closing the articulator. If the shape of the diamond is imperfect then it indicates a shift in the midline.

2. Errors in overjet and overbite:

Overjet is the amount of horizontal overlap and overbite is the amount of vertical overlap to explain in simple terms. In an ideal teeth arrangement, the overjet is around 2mm and the overbite is around 1mm. When viewed from the front and while assessing the overjet, it should be equal between the maxillary and mandibular anterior teeth. Same goes for overbite. Make sure the amount of these overlaps given are symmetrical.

3. Mandibular canine arrangement:

The arrangement of the mandibular canines differ from their maxillary counterparts. The long axis of the tooth should tilt towards the midline at the incisal third. There should be a slight distal rotation and care should be taken about maintaining the class I canine relation.

What are the common errors students make while arranging the maxillary posterior teeth?

While arranging the maxillary posterior teeth, the central grooves should follow the line from the point on the posterior land area to the canine tip. There should also be a small gap of maybe 0.5mm between the maxillary canine and the maxillary first premolar. This provides space for adjustment of occlusion after arrangement of mandibular posterior teeth.

Commonly seen errors:

1. Not maintaining the vertical stops:

This happens all too often unfortunately. Students are so held up in glass plate relations that they forget to maintain some part of the posterior-most portion of the occlusion rim as the vertical stop. We need this vertical stop to serve as a guide for our occlusal plane. Without a structure to limit the posterior plane, we will end up placing the posterior teeth too high or too low and to correct it is not easy.

So how do you go about correcting an incorrect occlusal plane? Well the first thing is to recreate the vertical stops. So add a stump of was where the vertical stop should've been and modify the height until the articulator can be closed with the newly formed vertical stop coming in flush contact with the mandibular occlusion rim. Keeping this as a guide, place the occlusion rim on a glass plate. Start by eliminating the posterior-most tooth which is not in the plane.

Continue to make corrections till the occlusal plane is restored.

2. Errors in glass plate relation:

If only a single tooth or two or more teeth are out of the occlusal plane, then when placing the occlusion rim in a centred manner on the glass plate, you will notice that the entire occlusion rim rocks anteriorly and posteriorly like a seesaw about a pivoting tooth. That tooth is the culprit that is out of the occlusal plane and needs to be corrected.

What are the common errors students make while arranging mandibular posterior teeth?

Common errors seen are:

1. Teeth arranged off centre:

Mandibular posterior teeth should be so arranged that the central grooves are aligned with the crest of the ridge. If not, it will affect the occlusion and esthetics of the arrangement.

2. Intercuspation adjustments:

While making occlusal adjustments to get a better intercuspation between maxillary and mandibular posterior teeth, take care not to alter the occlusal plane of the maxillary posterior teeth.

3. Lingual occlusion:

When viewed from the lingual aspect of the articulator, there should be intercuspal contact between maxillary palatal and mandibular lingual cusps.

Always remember:

1. Never ever compromise on the maxillary occlusal plane, that is the glass plate relation. If your maxillary posteriors are arranged correctly, automatically your mandibular posteriors will follow.
2. Preservation of the vertical stop posterior to the maxillary posterior teeth is an absolute must. A lot of students lose sight of this especially during the exam

and end up with a mess in the articulator.

3. Any changes being made to the mandibular posteriors has to be done carefully without causing any changes in the maxillary posterior teeth.

4. Always seal the teeth properly with wax and a heated instrument and make sure the wax has cooled sufficiently before proceeding to the next tooth. Otherwise the teeth will move and cause errors.

With that, your teeth arrangement is over. Way to go!

CHAPTER VII

Wax Up, Root Carving, Festooning & Sealing

Why do you need this exercise?

The success of a complete denture is in its function and esthetics. Esthetics is sometimes more important to the patient than function. If the complete denture appears to be a fake, then that is a failure on the part of the dentist. The wax on the trial denture base is a means of mimicking the soft tissues in the mouth and gives the denture a life-like appearance.

After the mammoth task of teeth arrangement, it's time to add on to the esthetics quotient of the denture bases. The process of wax up includes adding wax on to the trial denture bases to mimic the natural contours of a dentate mouth.

What are the common mistakes?

1. Inadequate addition of wax:

    In order to get a well contoured trial denture base, there has to be sufficient wax present to carve out. So make sure you add sufficient amount of wax along the teeth and the denture base area without changing the teeth position.

1. Excess addition of wax:

    On the other hand, make sure you remove all unnecessary wax from the trial bases. Excess wax adds to the weight of the prosthesis and makes the denture look bulky and unesthetic.

3. Over carving root forms:

If you run your tongue over the alveolar mucosa in your mouth you will notice two things. Root forms are most prominent in the maxillary canine and central incisor region. Everywhere else, including the posterior teeth regions, the root forms are more subtle. The same principle has to be applied while performing root carving for the trial denture bases as well. Over carved, prominent roots will not only look unesthetic, but will also be uncomfortable for your patient.

4. Bulbous gingival festooning:

Gingival festooning is an important part of esthetics of the complete denture. While carving the gingival margins, the tooth should look like they are emerging from the gingival tissues. Attention should also be given to the gingival zeniths. The maxillary centrals and canines have their gingival zeniths in the same height while for the maxillary lateral incisors it is lower and slightly towards the distal.

For the posteriors it reduces from premolars to molars. You can use a Lecron carver for this. Make use of a finger rest to gain better control of instrument movement. Angulating the carver while removing wax from around the tooth helps provide a more life-like appearance.

You can use the spoon end of the carver to carve out the root form depressions. Don't forget to pay attention to the interdental papilla area. Creating a butt joint between the teeth and the gingival wax creates the illusion of emergence. And finally while polishing, be careful not to overheat the wax as you will lose the carving details.

Once polishing is done, seal the trial bases onto the casts.

Make sure not to lose the occlusion and carving during these steps. Your trial bases are now ready for processing!

CHAPTER VIII

Cast Separation & Flasking

To separate the casts from the articulator, caution has to be observed, we must not damage the occlusion or the carving. Place the articulator sideways on a cloth and tap on the junction of the mounting plaster and the cast to separate the cast. You can use a wax knife and plaster mallet for this. Once you have the casts, set aside the articulator for later.

The next procedure is flasking.

Why do you need this exercise?

Flasking is an investing procedure in order to acrylise the complete denture. The procedure of flasking may sound simple: pour dental plaster or a mixture or dental plaster and dental stone into the flask, place the cast inside it and close the flask. However, errors that occur in this step can alter the vertical dimension of the final prosthesis. This basically means that the height of the prosthesis will be more than what was intended and although it may not make much of a difference in the preclinical aspect, during clinical procedure, it could even warrant the repetition of the entire prosthesis.

Some things to pay attention to while flasking:

1. Make sure the casts fit in the flask. If not, they must be trimmed to be accommodated within the flask.
2. Wetting the casts for 10 minutes in slurry water before flasking. A dry cast may dehydrate the investing material and reduce its strength leading to cracking during packing of heat cure acrylic resin. This could

cause increase in the vertical dimension.

3. Don't forget to line the inner surfaces of the flask as well as the surfaces of the casts with petroleum jelly.

4. After pouring the first layer of dental plaster in the flask, push the cast to touch the base of the flask leaving the posterior portion of the cast at the level of the upper margin of the flask.

5. After pouring the first layer of dental plaster in the flask, ensure that there is enough reinforcement around the maxillary tuberosity and retromandibular pad regions to protect them in the later stages of processing.

6. Before proceeding further, place the body component of the flask to ensure that the cast and teeth will not get in the way of flask closure. Sufficient space, around an inch should be available between the flask lid and teeth to avoid teeth movement or denture cracking during clamping of the flask.

7. Make sure there are no undercuts in the first pour to avoid locking of the second pour.

8. Wait for the dental plaster to set and dry before applying separating medium.

9. Make sure all components of the flask approximate perfectly without any gaps between them to avoid increase in vertical dimension or distortion.

10. Wait till the plaster is fully set before further procedures.

11. Make sure the clamp fits well over the flask and is tight enough to hold the components in place while the plaster sets as well as during further procedures.

And with that, you have completed flasking. On to the next step!

CHAPTER IX

Dewaxing & Packing

Why do you need this exercise?

The elimination of wax is very important before proceeding to pack the mould space with heat cure acrylic. Wax remnants left behind after improper dewaxing can interfere with the polymerisation process and act as a barrier between denture teeth and heat cure acrylic.

Packing is also an important step and proper knowledge and skill is necessary to ensure a well made prosthesis without porosities or any other processing errors.

How to dewax?

Once the plaster in the flasks has set, they can be kept in the dewaxing chamber. When the water boils, place the clamped flasks in the dewaxing chamber.

That way about 5 minutes is all it takes for the wax to melt. Once the flasks are removed, carefully open the flask and remove the remnants of wax. Make sure there are no wax residues left as it could hinder the polymerisation process.

After wax elimination, wait for the plaster to dry before applying separating medium again. To apply separating medium around the acrylic teeth, use a thin brush or a cotton piece wrapped around a Lecron carver.

Once the separating medium coating has dried, it is time to pack the mould space with heat cure acrylic.

How to mix heat cure acrylic?

Heat cure acrylic is mixed in a porcelain jar. Sift the polymer into the monomer till no more monomer is seen freely floating on the surface.

Close the lid of the jar to prevent evaporation of the rapid monomer evaporation. When it reaches the dough stage, which should take roughly 10 minutes, take the material from the porcelain jar and knead it with the fingers into a homogenous mass. In the dough stage, the material will easily pull away from the sides of the porcelain jar without sticking.

How much time do you have to work with the mix in dough stage?

According to ADA specifications, the dough stage will last for 5 minutes so you have ample time to pack the mould space effectively.

How to pack the heat cure acrylic resin?

Acrylic should be packed in the mould space of the flask and make sure it is filled completely. When the flask is closed, the cast portion of the flask will compress the acrylic into the mould space and the excess flash can be removed.

When tightening the clamp, apply the turns in increments, allowing the pressure to be dissipated. Leave the flasks clamped for bench curing for 30 minutes at least before commencing acrylisation.

CHAPTER X

Acrylisation, Deflasking, Finishing& Polishing

After bench curing for 30minutes to 60 minutes, the flasks can now be placed in the acrylisation unit.

Which curing cycle to follow?

The curing cycle usually followed is 74 degrees Celsius for 2 hours and 100 degrees Celsius for 1 hour. It is better to allow the water to gradually heat up while the flasks are present than to put the flasks in hot water. Make sure the temperature is maintained for the time period.

How and why to do bench cooling?

After curing cycle completion, remove the flasks and allow the flasks to sit for 30 minutes for bench cooling.

Do not attempt to cool the flasks suddenly as it can lead to warpage of the dentures. After 30 minutes, the flasks can be immersed in tap water for about 15 minutes.

After the flasks have completely cooled down, the flasks can be opened. Carefully pry open the flask with a wax knife. If you are unable to do so, you can gently tap the flask at the junction of the components using a mallet. Once separated, gently retrieve the master cast by tapping the sides of the flask.

How to retrieve the acrylised denture?

After the flasks have completely cooled down, the flasks can be opened. Carefully pry open the flask with a wax knife. If you are unable to do so, you can gently tap the flask at the junction of the components using a mallet. Once separated, gently retrieve the master cast by tapping the sides of the flask.

Retrieving the denture requires more caution. Very gently tap the top side of the denture flask component protecting the denture on the other side with your hand. Place the denture on the cast.

Remove any remnants of dental plaster or dental stone with a Lecron carver. Trim the excess acrylic flash with an acrylic trimmer. You can also use a tungsten carbide bur to trim away excess acrylic.

Pay special attention to the interdental spaces. You can use an explorer or any other fine tipped instrument to remove the lodged gypsum particles.

Use sand paper and/or emery paper to polish the acrylic surface. A final polish with pumice will give a shine to the acrylic.

And there you have it! A perfect set of acrylised complete dentures!

Congratulations!!!

References

REFERENCES:

1. Kumar S, Dagli RJ, Mathur A, Jain M, Prabu D, Kulkarni S. Perceived sources of stress amongst Indian dental students. Eur J Dent Educ. 2009;13(1):39-45.
2. Obrez A, Lee DJ, Organ-Boshes A, Yuan JC, Knight GW. A clinically oriented complete denture program for second-year dental students. J Dent Educ. 2009;73(10):1194-201.
3. Haralur SB, Al-Malki AE. Student perception about efficacy of preclinical fixed prosthodontic training to facilitate smooth transition to clinical context. J Educ Health Promot. 2014;3:73.
4. Manakil J, George R. Reviewing competency in dental education. International Journal of Dental Clinics. 2011;3(2):33-39.
5. Ebrahimi S, Kojuri J, Ashkani-Esfahani S. Early clinical experience: A way for preparing students for clinical setting. GMJ. 2012;1(2):42-47.
6. Divaris K, Barlow PJ, Chendea SA, Cheong WS, Dounis A, Dragan IF, et al. The academic environment: the students' perspective. Eur J Dent Educ. 2008;12 Suppl1:120-30.
7. Victoroff KZ, Hogan S. Students' perceptions of effective learning experiences in dental school: a qualitative study using a critical incident technique. J Dent Educ. 2006;70(2):124-32.
8. Ellinger CW, Rayson JH, Terry JM, Rahn AD (1975) Synopsis of complete dentures. 1st edn, Lea and Febicer, Philadelphia pp. 220-229.

9. Graig RG, Powers JM, Wataha JC (2000) Dental Materials properties and manipulation. 7th edn, Mosby, St Loui, USA pp. 211-217.

10. Harrison A, Huggett R, Murphy WM (1990) Complete dentures construction in general dental practice: An update of the 1970 survey, Br Dent J 169(6): 159-163.

11. Rudd RW, Rudd KD (2001) A review of 243 errors possible during the fabrication of a removable partial denture: Part I. J Prosthet Dent 86(3): 277-288.

12. Rudd RW, Rudd KD (2001) A review of 243 errors possible during the fabrication of a removable partial denture: Part II. J Prosthet Dent 2001;86:262-76

13. Rudd RW, Rudd KD (2001) A review of 243 errors possible during the fabrication of a removable partial denture: Part III. J Prosthet Dent 2001;86:277-88.

14. Shenoy, Nair; Phillips Science of Dental Materials, 1st South Asia Ed, 2014: pp 189-201

15. Shepard, W. L.: Denture bases processed from a fluid resin.J PROSTHET DENT 19:561, 1968.

16. Mirza, F. D.: Dimensional stability of acrylic resin dentures.J PROSTHET DENT 11:848, 1961.

17. Winkler, S., Ortman, H. R., Morris, H. F., and Plezia, R. A.: Processing changes in complete dentures constructed from pour resins. JAm Dent Assoc 82:349, 1971.

18. Grant, A. A., and Atkinson, H. F.: Comparison between dimensional accuracy of dentures with pour-type resin and with heat-processed materials. J PROSTHET DENT 26:296, 1971.

19. Payne SH. Contour and positioning. In: Moss SJ, editor.Esthetics. New York: Medcom Inc; 1973. pp. 50-54.

20. Swenson's complete dentures. The CV Mosby company:

6th ed. 1970.

21. Tench RW. A method for accurately remounting vulcanized dentures in the articulator for regrinding. Dent Dig 1920 May;26:286-298.

22. Prombonos A, Vlissidis P. Effects of position of artificial teeth and load levels on stress in the complete maxillary denture. J Prosthet Dent 2002 Oct;88(4):415-422 Morrow RM, Rudd KD, Rhoads JE. Dental laboratory pro- cedures. Vol. 1. Complete dentures: First South Asia edition. Elsevier; 2016.

23. Winkler S. Essentials of complete denture prosthodontics. 3rd ed. AITBS Publishers; 2015.

24. Zarb G, Hobkrik J, Eckert S, Jacob R. Boucher's prosthodontics treatment for edentulous patients. 13th ed. Mosby Publishers; 2013.

25. Jayalakshmi NS, Ravindra S, Nagaraj KR, Rupesh PL, Harshavardhan MP. Acceptable deviation between facial and dental midlines in dentate population. J Indian Prosthodont Soc 2013 Dec;13(4):473-477.

26. Heartwell Jr CM, Rahn AO. Syllabus of complete dentures. 4th ed.; 1986.

27. Monteith BD. Evaluation of a cephalometric method of occlu- sal plane orientation for complete dentures. J Prosthet Dent 1986 Jan;55(1):64-69.

28. EL Geriani AS, Davies AL, Winstanley RB. The gothic arch tracing and the upper canine teeth as guides in positioning of upper posterior teeth. J Oral Rehabil 1989 Sept;16(5): 481-490.

29. Beresin VE, Schiesser FJ. The neutral zone in complete den- tures. J Prosthet Dent 1976 Oct;36(4):356-367.

30. Darbar UE, Hugget R, Harrisson A. Stress analysis techniques in complete denture. J Dent 1999 Oct;22(5):259-264.

31. Keshvad A, Winstanley RB, Hooshmand T. Intercondylar width as a guide to setting up complete denture teeth. J Oral Rehabil 2000 Mar;27(3):217-226.

32. Sutton AF, McCord JF. A randomized control trial compar- ing anatomic, lingualised and zero degree occlusal forms for complete dentures. J Prosthet Dent 2007 May;97(5):292-298.

www.ingramcontent.com/pod-product-compliance
Lightning Source LLC
Chambersburg PA
CBHW040739120726
48007CB00008B/143